A CourseGuide for

Seeking Allah, Finding Jesus

Nabeel Qureshi

ZONDERVAN
REFLECTIVE

ZONDERVAN REFLECTIVE

A CourseGuide for Seeking Allah, Finding Jesus

Copyright © 2019 by Nabeel Qureshi

ISBN 978-0-310-11070-5 (softcover)

Requests for information should be addressed to:
Zondervan, *3900 Sparks Dr. SE, Grand Rapids, Michigan 49546*

Printed in the United States of America

CONTENTS

Introduction

Welcome to *A CourseGuide for Seeking Allah, Finding Jesus*. These guides were created for formal and informal students alike who want to engage deeper in biblical, theological, or ministry studies. We hope this guide will provide an opportunity for you to grow not only in your understanding, but also in your faith.

How to Use this Guide

This guide is meant to be used in conjunction with the book *Seeking Allah, Finding Jesus* and its corresponding videos, *Seeking Allah, Finding Jesus Video Study*. After you have read each chapter in the book and watched the accompanying video lesson, the materials in this guide will help you review and assess what you have learned. Application-oriented questions are included as well.

Each CourseGuide has been individually designed to best equip you in your studies, but in general, you can expect the following components. Most CourseGuides begin every chapter with a "You Should Know" section, which highlights key terminology, people, and facts to remember. This section serves as a helpful summary for directing your studies. Reflection questions, typically two to three per chapter, prompt you to summarize key points you've learned. Discussion questions invite you to an even deeper level of engagement. Finally, most chapters will end with a short quiz to test your retention. You can find the answer key to each quiz at the bottom of the page following it.

For Further Study

CourseGuides accompany books and videos from some of the world's top biblical and theological scholars. They may be used independently, or in small groups or classrooms, offering quality instruction to equip students for academic and ministry pursuits. If you would like to engage in further study with Zondervan's CourseGuides, the full lineup may be viewed online. After completing your studies with *A CourseGuide for Seeking Allah Finding Jesus*, we recommend moving on to *A CourseGuide for Evangelism in a Skeptical World* and *A CourseGuide for Apologetics at the Cross*.

CHAPTER 1

Called to Prayer

You Should Know

- *Shahada*: the central proclamation of Islam: "There is no god but Allah, and Muhammad is his messenger."

- Five Pillars of Islam: the fundamental practices required of all Muslims: reciting the shahada; praying the *salaat*; paying *zakat* to the poor; fasting during Ramadhan; and making pilgrimage to the Ka'ba to perform *Hajj*

- Six Articles of Faith: the fundamental Muslim beliefs: in the one God, Allah; in the unseen spiritual beings; that Allah sent prophets into the world; that he gave scripture to his prophets; that there will be a day of judgment; that Allah's decree is sovereign over the universe

- Main divisions in Islam: Shia and Sunni

- Ramadhan: the Muslim holy month

- *Hajj*: the annual pilgrimage to Mecca

- *Imam*: a leader of Muslims, usually referring to one who leads prayer at a mosque

- *Masjim*: a Muslim place of worship, often called a mosque

- *Jumaa*: the name for the Muslim Sabbath day

- *Du'aa*: Muslim prayers recited at specific occasions, as opposed to the ritual prayer called *Salaat*; these may be memorized or improvised

- *Assalaamo alaikum wa rahmutallah wa barakaathu*: an extended Muslim greeting meaning, "The peace of Allah and his mercy and blessings be upon you."

Reflection Questions

1. Islam is more than just an identity; it is a worldview that impacts how Muslims see the world. How does your own worldview impact how you see the world?

2. Summarize the Five Pillars of Islam. Can you appreciate or do you resonate with any of them? If so, which ones?

3. Describe and explain a number of the religious activities and rituals of Muslims, including congregational life and daily prayers. Which ones do you resonate with and/or practice?

Essay Question

1. As you begin this course, what are your impressions of Islam? What shaped those impressions? Nabeel says that the exceptional blend of love, humility, hospitality, and perseverance can overcome barriers blocking Muslim immigrants from understanding Christians. Which ones might you need to grow in or ask God to help you cultivate in order to reach out to Muslims?

Quiz

1. What is the essential message of Islam?
   a) Salvation by Allah
   b) Submission to Allah
   c) Friendship of Allah
   d) Judgment by Allah

2. What does *Muslim* mean?
   a) One who is saved
   b) One who submits
   c) One who is befriended
   d) One who is judged

3. The Shahada is the central proclamation of Islam. What does it say?

a) "There is no god but Allah, and Muhammad is one of his messengers."
b) "There is no god but Allah, and Muhammad is his messenger."
c) "There is no god but Muhammad, and Allah is his messenger."
d) "There is no god but Allah."

4. (T/F) Islam is more than just a set of beliefs, it's who Muslims are; Islam is an identity, not just what Muslims believe. Muslims don't separate their *self* from their *beliefs*.

5. Muslims consider Muhammad's life exemplary, and devout Muslims emulate him as much as possible. To do so, Muslims learn stories about his life from:

a) The Quran
b) Books of Sirah
c) Hadith
d) B & C
e) None of the above

6. (T/F) Muslims believe Judaism and Christianity became corrupted, and Islam is the only incorruptible faith.

7. According to Islam, what is our human problem, and what do we need most?

a) Every person is basically good and needs the encouragement to do the right thing.
b) Every person is a sinner and needs to be saved by the grace of God.
c) Everyone is ignorant and needs proper guidance to follow and submit to God.
d) None of the above

8. How should we determine if Muslims are *true* Muslims?

a) If someone belongs to the dominant Sunni sect of Islam
b) If someone follows Muhammad and declares the Shahada
c) If someone lives in the Middle East
d) All of the above

9. Sharia is Islamic law that explains how you should live in order to submit to Allah. From what source is it derived?

    a) The teachings of the Quran only
    b) The teachings of the *hadith* only
    c) A composite understanding of the Quran and *hadith*
    d) Neither the Quran nor the *hadith*

10. (T/F) At the end of the day, the basic worldview of Islam is the same: Allah wants us to submit to him and follow the law he's given, *sharia*.

CHAPTER 2

An Ambassador for Islam

You Should Know

- Christianity and Islam have roughly analogous beliefs in regard to monotheism, spiritual and physical realms, angels and demons, good and evil, a final judgment, heaven and hell, the inspiration of scriptures, and many more peripheral beliefs.

- Regarding Jesus, there are two issues on which Muslims particularly disagree with Christians: that Jesus died on the cross and that Jesus claimed to be God.

- *Sahih Bukhari*: a classical collection of *hadith*, often considered by Sunnis as the most trustworthy accounts of Muhammad's life

- From marital rites to martial restrictions, commercial laws to civil suits, the vast majority of sharia law and the Islamic way of life is derived from the *hadith*.

- *Isnad*: the chain of transmission for a particular *hadith*

- *Sahih Sittah*: the sixth book of *hadith* that Sunni Muslims consider most authentic

- Doctrine of abrogation: the belief that teachings and verses of the Quran have been repealed, usually by later Quranic revelation

- Islamic cultures tend to establish people of high status as authorities, whereas the authority in Western culture is reason itself.

- The earliest historical records show that Muhammad launched offensive military campaigns and used violence at times to accomplish his purposes. The peaceful practice of Islam hinges on later, often Western, interpretations of Muhammad's teachings, whereas the more violent variations of Islam are deeply rooted in orthodoxy and history.

- Muhammad used the term *jihad* in both spiritual and physical contexts, but the physical *jihad* is the one Muhammad strongly emphasizes.

Reflection Questions

1. The heritage of many Muslims is often a deterrent for many would-be friends in the West, sometimes leading to loneliness. How might it look in your own life to not let such a heritage deter you from befriending Muslims you know?

2. As we've seen from this session, there are some roughly analogous beliefs that Christians and Muslims share. What are they? How do you think these commonalities might be helpful in creating dialogue with Muslims you may get to know?

3. When it comes to the question about whether Islam is a religion of peace, how have you yourself answered this question? How would you answer it after this session?

Essay Question

1. What are the differences between Islam and Christianity regarding beliefs about Jesus and Muhammad? After this lesson, can you understand and appreciate why what Muslims believe about Jesus and Muhammed are the most sensitive differences between Islam and Christianity? Explain.

Quiz

1. (T/F) Muslim immigrants from the East have very few differences from Muslim children born in the West.

2. Which nations are populated by the most Muslims?

   a) Indonesia, Pakistan, India, and Bangladesh
   b) Saudi Arabia, Iraq, Iran, and Syria
   c) England, France, Germany, and Turkey
   d) Morocco, Libya, Tunisia, and Egypt

3. There are simply too many barriers for Muslim immigrants to understand Christians and the West by sheer circumstance. Only with what can we overcome these barriers?

   a) Love
   b) Humility
   c) Hospitality
   d) Persistence
   e) All of the above

4. (T/F) Almost universally, second generation Muslims see the world as Western and yet still align themselves with Islam.

5. Islam and Christianity have roughly analogous beliefs in:

   a) Monotheism
   b) Angels and demons
   c) Good and evil
   d) Heaven and hell
   e) The inspiration of scriptures
   f) All of the above

6. What is the most sensitive difference between Islam and Christianity?

   a) Their views of Jesus and Muhammad
   b) Their views of the Bible and the Quran
   c) Their views of angels and demons
   d) Their views of sin and salvation

7. Regarding Jesus, on what two issues do Muslims particularly disagree with Christians, and the Quran specifically denies?

   a) Jesus died on the cross and rose from the dead
   b) Jesus died on the cross and claimed to be God

   c) Jesus claimed to be God and the Messiah
   d) Jesus claimed to be God and performed a number of miracles

8. (T/F) There is no overestimating the importance of *hadith* in the Islamic world.

9. One of the biggest differences between the West and the East is the honor-shame paradigm, versus the innocence-guilt paradigm. In the honor-shame paradigm:

   a) Right and wrong is viewed through the lens of what society and authority thinks are right and wrong.
   b) Positional authority yields a society that determines right and wrong based on honor and shame.
   c) Authority is derived from individual reason; each person is expected to critically examine his own course of action, doing what he knows to be right or wrong.
   d) A & B

10. (T/F) When it comes to the question of whether Islam is a religion of peace, defining the religion more traditionally as the system of beliefs and practices taught by Muhammad, the answer is ambiguous at best.

CHAPTER 3

Testing the New Testament

You Should Know

- Jeremiah 31:31, 33: "'The days are coming,' declares the Lord, 'when I will make a new covenant with the people of Israel and with the people of Judah.' 'This is the covenant I will make with the people of Israel after that time,' declares the Lord. 'I will put my law in their minds and write it on their hearts. I will be their God, and they will be my people.'"

- John 16:13: "But when he, the Spirit of truth, comes, he will guide you into all the truth. He will not speak on his own; he will speak only what he hears, and he will tell you what is yet to come."

- Muslim beliefs about the Quran: Muhammad was a conduit through which Allah revealed the Quran; Muhammad didn't write the Quran

- Characteristics of the Quran: one book, recorded by one person, at one time, in one voice

- The Bible is the "what" of the Christian faith and belief.

- Muslims believe the Gospels were initially inspired by the Word of God, but have since been changed; they are the books of the Bible Muslims are most concerned about.

- Muslims don't generally like Paul because they believe he hijacked Christianity; they believe he wasn't a true disciple, remade Jesus into God, and changed everything Jesus taught.

- Textual criticism: a field of biblical studies that analyzes original ancient manuscripts through comparison to discover alterations

- Biblical inspiration: the belief that God inspired the original message of the Bible, rather than merely the original words, allowing the Bible to be translated

- *Injil*: the book that Muslims believe Allah sent to Jesus, often considered to be the Gospels of the New Testament

Reflection Questions

1. Explain what is meant by the statement that the Bible is not the "why" of Christian belief. What do you think about this idea, and why is this important?

2. Why do you think Muslims generally take issue mainly with the New Testament, rather than with the whole Bible? Why do you think Muslims have such a difficult time with the New Testament when they are comparing it to the Quran?

3. Do you think you can be confident in the New Testament? Why or why not? Why do you think it's important to ask our Muslim friends to substantiate their claims about the New Testament and look at the context of contested passages?

Essay Question

1. Summarize and explain the textual validity of both the Quran and the New Testament. When comparing the Quran and the Bible, do you think Muslims can be confident in their own holy book in the same way we can in ours? Explain.

Quiz

1. (T/F) The Bible is not the "why" of Christian belief; it's the "what" of Christian belief.

2. Generally speaking, the issue Muslims have with the Bible is not with the whole Bible. What they have problems with is usually:

a) The New Testament
b) The idea that the Trinity is a real teaching
c) The idea that Jesus said he would die on the cross
d) All of the above

3. What do Muslims believe about Muhammad's relationship to the Quran?

a) Muhammad wrote the Quran, much like the authors of the Bible.
b) Muhammad discovered the Quran hidden in the ground, much like the Book of Mormon.
c) Muhammad was a conduit through which Allah revealed the Quran.
d) A & C

4. What is the ultimate goal of Muslims when it comes to the Bible?

a) Seeing the Bible is reliable
b) Seeing the Bible is truthful
c) Seeing the Bible is inerrant
d) Seeing the Bible is inspired
e) All of the above

5. (T/F) Muslims have never thought that the New Testament was inspired.

6. Within how many years of Jesus's life have are we able to date individual manuscripts of the Gospels and the rest of the New Testament?

a) 400 years
b) 100 years
c) 250 years
d) 500 years

7. Why can we be confident that at no point were there any major introductions of new doctrines or teachings into the Bible?

a) We can go back to the earliest manuscripts.
b) God has revealed it to us.
c) The Church has examined it.
d) We really can't.

8. When Muslims ask which versions of the Bible (i.e. NIV, ESV, NKJV) is the most accurate, why can we say with confidence that they can turn to any of them?

    a) They say the same thing.
    b) They rely on the same manuscripts.
    c) They communicate the same message.
    d) All of the above

9. Which verses are later additions and generally considered by most scholars not to have originally been part of the Bible?

    a) Mark 16:9–10 and John 7:53–8:11
    b) Genesis 1:26:27 and Exodus 20:1–17
    c) Romans 3:23 and Colossians 1:15–20
    d) Matthew 5:1–7:29 and John 2:1–12

10. Why can't Muslims be confident that the Quran they have dates back to Muhammad himself?

    a) Khalifa Uthman was a liar.
    b) All of the earliest manuscripts are lost or were destroyed.
    c) Muhammad was illiterate and couldn't have written a book.
    d) All of the above

CHAPTER 4

Coming to the Crux

You Should Know

- Jesus's death and resurrection are the "why" of the Christian faith and beliefs.

- The Quran insists Jesus was neither crucified nor killed. The litmus test between Islam and Christianity is the issue of whether Jesus died on the cross.

- Swoon theory: the belief by Muslims and others that Jesus didn't actually die on the cross, but he survived; instead, he gave only the appearance that he died by falling unconscious

- Appearance theory: the most ancient Muslim belief that Jesus was never placed on the cross in the first place; someone else who looked like Jesus or received the face of Jesus from Allah was placed on the cross in his stead

- The Muslim dilemma of Jesus's death: if Allah sustained Jesus (swoon theory) or replaced Jesus (appearance theory) then Allah was actively involved in deceiving people into believe the resurrection; Allah, then, was the one who started Christianity

- Criterion of early testimony: a principle of the historical method that posits that early accounts of an event are more likely to be accurate than later accounts, all else being equal

- Criterion of multiple attestation: a principle of the historical method that posits that a recorded event is more likely to be historically accurate if it is recorded in multiple independent sources

- Facts of the resurrection: Jesus died by crucifixion; Jesus's disciples truly believed he had risen from the dead; enemies of Jesus believed that he had risen from the dead

- Hallucination theory: the most famous hypothesis explaining the resurrection by non-Christians, suggesting that the disciples and multiple eyewitnesses had experienced a mass hallucination of his return

- Stolen body theory: a common hypothesis explaining the resurrection by non-Christians, suggesting somebody (often the disciples) had stolen Jesus's body from the tomb, leading people to believe he had risen

Reflection Questions

1. What is meant by the statement that the death and resurrection of Jesus is the "why" of the Christian faith, rather than the "what"? Explain.

2. Summarize and describe the *minimal facts* approach to the resurrection, as proposed by Dr. Gary Habermas and Dr. Michael Licona.

3. Nabeel argued that if we can determine one of the three major arguments of the Christian faith—Jesus claimed to be God; Jesus died on the cross; Jesus rose from dead—are false, then the whole case for Christianity falls apart. Explain these claims and why Nabeel might be right.

Essay Question

1. Compare and contrast the Christian and Islamic positions regarding the death of Jesus. Why can you be confident that history is squarely in favor of the Christian claim that Jesus died by crucifixion? What about the Islamic position presented in the Quran regarding Jesus, death?

Quiz

1. (T/F) If the Bible is the "what" of the Christian faith, the death and resurrection is the "why" of the Christian faith.

2. What do the Quran and Islamic faith say about the death of Jesus?

    a) That he did not die on the cross; he was not crucified.
    b) That he died a different way than crucifixion on the cross.
    c) That he did in fact die on the cross, like the Gospels say.
    d) None of the above

3. Among the scholars who study Jesus's life, how many agree that Jesus died by crucifixion?

    a) There's virtual unanimity.
    b) There's no consensus.
    c) There's hardly any agreement.
    d) No one says this

4. (T/F) The process of crucifixion is a very nearly impossible experience to survive, which is why virtually nobody has suggested that Jesus did not die by crucifixion.

5. One major view Muslims have regarding the death of Jesus is that he 'swooned.' What is this theory?

    a) Jesus disappeared on the cross.
    b) Jesus fell unconscious on the cross and survived.
    c) Jesus wasn't put on the cross to begin with.
    d) Jesus's face on the cross was put on someone else by Allah.
    e) C & D

6. What is the second major view that Muslims have regarding Jesus's death?

    a) Jesus disappeared on the cross.
    b) Jesus fell unconscious on the cross and survived.
    c) Jesus wasn't put on the cross to begin with.
    d) Jesus's face was put on someone else by Allah.
    e) C & D

7. What must Muslims exercise if they believe either that Jesus survived the cross or Allah put his face on somebody else?

    a) Faith
    b) Doubt
    c) Ignorance
    d) Disbelief

8. What facts point toward the resurrection of Jesus that even non-Christian scholars believe?

    a) Jesus died by crucifixion.
    b) Jesus's disciples truly believed that he had risen from the dead.
    c) Jesus's enemies believed that he had risen from the dead.
    d) All of the above

9. What are the most famous alternative hypotheses that non-Christians, including Muslims, offer to explain the resurrection account?

    a) A mass hallucination
    b) A political conspiracy
    c) Zealous followers stole the body
    d) A & C

10. What is a litmus test that shows whether a Muslim is actually approaching evidence historically, or by faith alone?

    a) The case for Jesus's death by crucifixion
    b) The case for Jesus's resurrection
    c) The case for Jesus's virgin birth
    d) The case for Jesus's miracles

CHAPTER 5

Jesus: Mortal Messiah or Divine Son of God?

You Should Know

- Isaiah 7:14: "Therefore the Lord himself will give you a sign: The virgin will conceive and give birth to a son, and will call him Immanuel."

- John 1:14: "The Word became flesh and made his dwelling among us. We have seen his glory, the glory of the one and only Son, who came from the Father, full of grace and truth."

- Mark 2:10: "But I want you to know that the Son of Man has authority on earth to forgive sins."

- Incarnation: this historic Christian belief that God became human and entered our world in the person of Jesus Christ

- *Asbab-al-Nuzul*: a body of Islamic literature purporting to detail the circumstances of specific Quranic revelations

- *Nafl*: optional prayers designed to invoke the help of Allah or draw the worshiper closer to him

- *Khutba*: a sermon, usually the Muslim Sabbath sermon on Friday

- Christology: an interpretation of Jesus's nature, identity, or role; for example, the Quran has a lower Christology than John, since he is just human in the former yet divine in the latter.

- Son of Man: a prophetic vision in Daniel 7 of Jesus Christ, who is God but looks like a human and was given authority, glory, and sovereign power; is worshiped by all nations and people of every language; and will have dominion and a kingdom that will never pass or be destroyed

- Hypostatic union: the historic Christian doctrine describing the personal union of Jesus's divinity and humanity; Jesus is fully God and fully human, united together in the one God-man person

Reflection Questions

1. What do Muslims believe about Jesus? Why is it important to your discussions with Muslims to understand what they generally believe and don't believe?

2. Christians often take it for granted that Jesus claimed to be God, yet the Quran condemns believing in Jesus as God. Why is this an important thing to keep in mind when discussing Jesus's deity with Muslims? How would you respond to this claim denying that Jesus himself claimed to be God? Briefly explain using Scripture.

3. What does it tell you about the Christian faith that one of the earliest teachings of the Church is that Jesus is Yahweh? What does it mean to you and your faith that Jesus is God—that God was born as a real human and took on a human nature?

Essay Question

1. What is the Islamic perspective on God, specifically the incarnation? Why do we need to show Muslims that the Islamic conception of God is not the one we're talking about when we talk about Jesus and his deity? How can you introduce them to the biblical God, what he has done, and how we see him?

Quiz

1. (T/F) The most common issue in Muslim Christian dialogue and chief concern for Muslims is their belief that Jesus never claimed to be God.

2. How do Muslims explain Jesus's miracles?

    a) They were all accomplished by God's permission, and by a power intrinsic to Jesus.

    b) They were all accomplished by God's permission, not by any power intrinsic to Jesus.

    c) They were never accomplished in the first place, but were legends crafted by his followers.

    d) All of the above

3. (T/F) The Bible and the Quran are pretty much alike, so it is fine that Muslims try to interpret the Bible as they would the Quran.

4. When Christians claim Jesus was God, Muslims often respond by saying:

    a) Jesus said he could do no miracles in Galilee; how can God not do miracles?

    b) Jesus grew in wisdom and in stature; how does it make sense that God can grow in wisdom?

    c) Jesus said he does not know something that the father knows; how can God not know what God knows?

    d) All of the above

5. What is an Old Testament example of God entering into his world, showing that he wasn't doing something new with Jesus?

    a) In Genesis 18 and 19, Yahweh appeared before Abraham.

    b) In Exodus 24, Moses and the elders of Israel had a meal with Yahweh.

    c) In Genesis 32, Jacob wrestled with God.

    d) All of the above

6. Where in Mark do we find evidence of Jesus's deity?

    a) The arrival of John the Baptist, preparing the way of the Messiah

    b) Jesus's declaration that he forgives sins and is Lord of the Sabbath

    c) Jesus's calming of the wind and waves

    d) A & C

    e) All of the above

7. What two Old Testament passages did Jesus reference when he claimed to be the Son of Man in Mark 14:62?

  a) Genesis 1:26–27 and Genesis 12:1–3
  b) Daniel 7:13–14 and Psalm 110:1
  c) Isaiah 7 and 9
  d) Deuteronomy 6:4–5 and Jeremiah 29:11

8. Why did the Jewish religious leaders charge Jesus with blasphemy in Mark 14:64?

  a) Jesus did miracles
  b) Jesus taught opposing views
  c) Jesus claimed to be God
  d) Jesus ate with sinners
  e) B & C

9. (T/F) When Jesus said, "You will see the Son of Man sitting at the right hand of the power and coming with the clouds of heaven" in Mark 14:62, he was quoting Daniel 7:13–14 and saying, "I am that person who deserves to be worshipped by all people."

10. In which Gospels do we find Jesus claiming to be God?

  a) Matthew and Luke, but not Mark and John
  b) Matthew, Luke, and John; not Mark
  c) Matthew, Luke, and Mark; not John
  d) All four gospels

ANSWER KEY

1. T, 2. B, 3. F, 4. D, 5. D, 6. E, 7. B, 8. C, 9. T, 10. D

CHAPTER 6

The Case for the Gospel

You Should Know

- Romans 10:9: "If you declare with your mouth, 'Jesus is Lord,' and believe in your heart that God raised him from the dead, you will be saved."

- Genesis 1:26–27: "Then God said, 'Let us make mankind in our image, in our likeness, so that they may rule over the fish in the sea and the birds in the sky, over the livestock and all the wild animals, and over all the creatures that move along the ground.' So God created mankind in his own image, in the image of God he created them; male and female he created them."

- Deuteronomy 6:4–5: "Hear, O Israel: The Lord our God, the Lord is one. Love the Lord your God with all your heart and with all your soul and with all your strength."

- *Tauheed*: the Islamic doctrine of Allah's absolute unity and self-reliance

- The message of the Trinity: there is one God who existed from eternity past in a community of three, interacting in a community of selfless love; the triune God is the essence of love

- *Dawah*: the practice of inviting people to Islam

- Substitutionary atonement: the doctrine that Jesus is able to take and pay for the sins of man

- Essential doctrine of the gospel: Jesus is God; Jesus died on the cross; Jesus rose from the dead

- Three things Muslims deny about Jesus: Jesus is God (and claimed to be God); Jesus died on the cross; Jesus rose from the dead

- The gospel message: God loves us despite our sins, so much that he willingly entered into this world to suffer alongside us, take our sins upon himself, die on the cross on our behalf, and rise from the dead so we can have faith in him and in our own resurrection eternally

Reflection Questions

1. Why do you think people want signs that give evidence for Jesus's claims, as the crowds did in Matthew 12? Which of Jesus's signs in the Gospels do you think is most important? Why?

2. The case for the gospel is made by the historic validity of Jesus's deity, death, and resurrection. Why do you think all three are crucial to dialoguing with Muslims?

3. What does the Quran say Allah's posture is toward sinners? How do you think this might impact Muslims? What does the gospel say instead?

Essay Question

1. Summarize and describe the doctrines of the Trinity and salvation. How do they contrast with Islam? Why are they so important to a conversation with a Muslim about the gospel?

Quiz

1. What do Muslims believe about Jesus?
   a) He is the Messiah, he is God, he died on the cross
   b) He is chosen by God (Messiah), he is virgin born, he is a miracle-worker
   c) He is God, he died on the cross, he rose again
   d) None of the above

2. The case for the gospel is strong, but Muslims often challenge its message in two ways. What are they?

   a) Creation and evolution
   b) The Trinity and God's grace
   c) Jesus's death and resurrection
   d) None of the above

3. Which Islamic doctrine is antithetical to the doctrine of the Trinity?

   a) *Shahada*
   b) *Jihad*
   c) *Tauheed*
   d) *Sharia*

4. (T/F) When the Quran says that God is not three, it is really not denying the Trinity that we orthodox Christians believe; it's denying the heretical Trinity.

5. What is the definition of the Trinity, according to the orthodox Christian faith?

   a) God is one being in three persons.
   b) God is three persons.
   c) God is only one being.
   d) None of the above

6. Muslims often point out that the word "Trinity" isn't in the Bible. What important phrase that's central to the Islamic view of Allah isn't in the Quran?

   a) *Tauheed*, the Islamic doctrine of Allah's absolute unity and self-reliance
   b) The two phrases of the *Shahada*
   c) All of the above
   d) None of the above

7. When Jesus said in the Gospel of John that the Father is greater than him, he's referring to:

   a) Their separate essence
   b) Their separate roles

c) Their separate forms
d) All of the above

8. The Quran insists that, "No one who bears a burden can carry the burdens of another"? Christians would actually agree with this. Why does Jesus fit the criteria Muslims themselves give for carrying the burdens of our sins?

a) Jesus was sinless.
b) Jesus was a good man.
c) Jesus was a good teacher.
d) Jesus was a nomad.

9. According to the Christian faith, how can God be both infinitely merciful and infinitely just at the same time, while also forgiving every single person?

a) He instituted the sacrificial system.
b) He outlined religious rituals to fulfill.
c) He commanded a series of laws to obey.
d) He accepted his penalty for sin by paying the penalty for sinful humanity; he himself took it on.

10. (T/F) Allah, a monadic God, did not live in a community in eternity past; he was just one, he had nothing to love. A God of intrinsic selfless, self-sacrificial love can only come from the doctrine of the Trinity.

CHAPTER 7

The Truth about Muhammad

You Should Know

- Muhammad is the man who embodies Islam, a symbol for the whole of Islamic civilization, their pride and identity; the chief messenger of Allah to whom he gave his final revelation to humanity, the Quran. Mecca was the birthplace of Muhammad in 570 AD.

- *al-Insan al-Kamil*: an honorific title of Islamic theology given to Muhammad; translated "the man who has attained perfection"

- Deuteronomy 18:18: an Old Testament passage often cited by Muslims showing the foretelling of the coming of a prophet like Moses, believed to be Muhammad; "I will raise up for them a prophet like you from among their fellow Israelites, and I will put my words in his mouth. He will tell them everything I command him."

- John 16:12–13: the New Testament passage often cited by Muslims showing that Jesus pointed forward to a promised counselor, believed to be Muhammad; "I have much more to say to you, more than you can now bear. But when he, the Spirit of truth, comes, he will guide you into all the truth. He will not speak on his own; he will speak only what he hears, and he will tell you what is yet to come."

- The first biography of the life of Muhammad was *Sirat Rasul Allah*, the written by Ibn Ishaq 140 years after his death; *Sirat Rasul Allah* means, "The Life of the Prophet." Ibn Hishan saved and transmitted edited portions of Muhammad's original biography, *Sirat Rasul Allah*; he didn't save it all and left portions out.

- *Sirah* is literature similar to a biography; it recounts Muhammad's life in chronological order in story form. *Hadith* are individual accounts of Muhammad's words and actions recorded in tradition, collected 200–250 years after Muhammad died. *Isnad* is the chain of transmission for a particular *hadith*.

- "How do we know?" is the most devastating and important question to ask whether historical documents (like the Quran, *hadith*, and *Sirah*) are trustworthy.

- *La-iqraha fi-deen*: a passage from the Quran, translated "there is no compulsion in religion;" often cited to suggest Muhammad did not spread religion by the sword

- Quran 4:24: "Forbidden for you are women already married, except such as your right hands possess. Allah has enjoined this on you."

Reflection Questions

1. Why might it be important to keep in mind that Muhammad is the symbol of Islamic pride and identity? What does this suggest about the Muslim faith, and how might that impact how you dialogue with them?

2. Are the Islamic sources about Muhammad's life historically valid? Explain. How might the fact that the stories about Muhammad weren't ultimately collected until 200–250 years after he died be important?

3. Why is the question "How do you know that?" such an important, "devastating question," as Nabeel puts it? Why should you use it when dialoguing with Muslims about their faith?

Essay Question

1. In your own words, retell the story of Muhammad and the beginning of Islam. When it comes to dialoguing with Muslims about their faith, why might it be important for you to know about the contours of Muhammad's life?

Quiz

1. What features of Muslim life find their core in the person of Muhammad?

   a) Religion
   b) Culture
   c) Heritage
   d) Identity
   e) All of the above

2. Which two biblical passages do Muslim apologists reference to advance the argument that Islam is the culmination of the Old Testament and New Testament?

   a) Deuteronomy 18:18; John 16:12–13
   b) Deuteronomy 6:4–5; John 3:16
   c) Genesis 12:1–3; Luke 4:18–19
   d) None of the above

3. From what Islamic sources do we understand the life of Muhammad, what he did and said?

   a) The Quran
   b) *Sirah* literature
   c) *Hadith* literature
   d) All of the above
   e) B & C

4. When was the first time anyone wrote anything about Muhammad's life after he died, when Ibn Ishaq wrote *Sirat Rasul Allah*?

   a) 20 years
   b) 140 years
   c) 60 years
   d) 245 years

5. (T/F) The earliest biography that we have of Muhammad's life is actually an edited biography, because the original one had things in it that people considered fabrications.

6. Muslims tend to trust *hadith* literature because of this special hallmark:

a) It was written by reliable persons.

b) It was written early.

c) It has a compelling story.

d) It has a chain of transmission.

7. Why aren't the *hadith* reliable witnesses of Muhammad's life and activity?

a) The sources are too late.

b) We can't be sure how accurate the stories are.

c) We can't test the character of those who passed along the stories.

d) All of the above

8. People talk about Muhammad's life and Jesus's life as if we can be equally certain about what Jesus did and what Muhammad did. But what major difference is there between the two accounts?

a) Jesus's life was inspired.

b) Jesus's life was written down by his disciples.

c) Jesus's life was written in Greek.

d) All of the above

9. What kinds of activities are recorded about the life of Muhammad?

a) He did some good things for women's rights.

b) He taught people to take care of widows and orphans.

c) He ordered the beheading of 500–800 Jewish men.

d) He allowed his followers to use conquered women as sex slaves.

e) All of the above

10. When you bring up violent aspects of Muhammad's life, you should:

a) Be honest because it's true, and the truth is what matters.

b) Don't bring it up, because it doesn't matter.

c) Don't bring it up, because it isn't true.

d) Be careful because it will be seen as an attack on Muhammad, and you could lose the relationship.

ANSWER KEY

1. E, 2. A, 3. E, 4. B, 5. T, 6. D, 7. D, 8. B, 9. E, 10. D

CHAPTER 8

The Holiness of the Quran

You Should Know

- The Quran is the perfectly preserved inspired words of Allah dictated verbatim to Muhammad through the archangel Gabriel; the closest thing to the incarnation of Allah, paralleling Jesus's incarnation.

- Khalifa Uthman was an early supreme leader who ordered that the Quran be standardized, recalling the previous copies of Muhammad's widow; he edited it, copied it, and distributed it to each Muslim province; he then ordered all other Quran materials, whether written in fragmentary manuscripts or whole copies, to be destroyed by fire. The *Hafs-an-Asim* is a particular reading of the Quran that was printed in 1923, becoming the version used most commonly in the world by Muslims today.

- Five arguments of Islam for divine inspiration of Quran:
    a) Inimitability
    b) perfect textual preservation
    c) scientific truths
    d) fulfilled prophecy
    e) mathematical patterns

- *al-Furqan al-Haqq*: a book of Christian teachings written in Quranic style, challenging the argument of inimitability; translated "the true measure of discernment"

- Textual preservation: the Islamic argument that not one dash, not one letter of the Quran has ever been changed; believed to show that God has been guarding the text from its inception, according to Quran 15:9: "Surely We have revealed the Reminder [Quran] and We will most surely be its guardian."

- Bucailleism: the technique of referring to the Quran for miraculously advanced scientific truths in order to defend its divine origin

- Doctrine of abrogation: the belief that teachings and verses of the Quran have been repealed, usually by later Quranic revelations

Reflection Questions

1. What are the major differences between how Muslims view the Quran and how Christians view the Bible in terms of the meaning of the words and message? How does the Islamic view of the Quran compare to the Christian view of Jesus, and why might this be important?

2. What is the Muslim understanding of the process of Muhammad receiving the Quran and then propagating it? Briefly explain the history behind how the Quran came to be in its current form.

3. A good response to the Quran is actually being confident in your knowledge of and familiarity with the biblical text. Are you confident in the Bible? How familiar with it are you? What do you need to grow in this confidence for the sake of your outreach?

Essay Question

1. What are the five arguments Muslims use to defend the divine inspiration of the Quran? Summarize and describe them, then explain why they are deficient.

Quiz

1. (T/F) The Quran really is the "why" of Islam, not just the "what." It is the reason Muslims believe in the teachings of Islam.

2. Like Christians, how do Muslims generally use the Quran?

    a) Personal devotions

    b) Liturgical purposes

    c) Daily prayers

    d) All of the above

    e) B & C

3. Rather than the Quran being analogous to the Bible, to what Christian concept is it comparable instead?

    a) The Trinity

    b) Jesus's incarnation

    c) Yahweh

    d) The Ten Commandments

4. What do Muslims believe about the Quran?

    a) The verses of the Quran have already been inscribed in tablets in heaven.

    b) Muhammad received packets of revelation from Gabriel orally.

    c) Muhammad had scribes write down more or less what he received so people could recite it.

    d) All of the above

    e) B & C

5. (T/F) The manner in which Muslims believe the Quran came to them is comparable to how the New Testament was propagated.

6. How many years after Mohammad's death was the Quran standardized?

    a) 2 years

    b) 200 years

    c) 60 years

    d) 20 years

7. After the Quran was finally standardized into a single version, what happened to all other versions and manuscripts?

    a) They were preserved.

    b) They were hidden.

c) They were destroyed.

d) They were buried.

8. (T/F) What Islam claims is that the meaning of the Quran has not changed, rather than insisting not one letter or word has changed.

9. What scientific revelation is contained in the Quran?

a) That sperm is produced between a man's backbone and his ribs.

b) Descriptions of the stages of embryonic development

c) The Quran is oftentimes wrong about science, or statements about its scientific content are often read into the text.

d) A & B

10. The best Christian response to the Quran is:

a) Being familiar with the Quran after having read it

b) Being confident in the Bible and familiar with it

c) Having arguments prepared to refute the Quran

d) All of the above

CHAPTER 9

Faith in Doubt

You Should Know

- Romans 5:8: "But God demonstrates his own love for us in this: While we were still sinners, Christ died for us."

- Mark 8:34–35: "Then he called the crowd to him along with his disciples and said: 'Whoever wants to be my disciple must deny themselves and take up their cross and follow me. For whoever wants to save their life will lose it, but whoever loses their life for me and for the gospel will save it.'"

- Matthew 7:7–8: "Ask and it will be given to you; seek and you will find; knock and the door will be opened to you. For everyone who asks receives; the one who seeks finds; and to the one who knocks, the door will be opened."

- Honor-shame is an aspect of many Eastern cultures wherein social authority impacts personal actions; what matters is how an action is viewed by society, what society and authority thinks are right and wrong; a person doesn't want to bring shame or lose honor.

- Apologetics: arguments in favor of the Christian faith designed to break down barriers to help position people to make a decision to pursue God or not

- Cost for Muslims accepting the gospel:
  a) immediately ostracized from community
  b) rejection by friends and family
  c) brings shame to family
  d) fear they might be wrong
  e) and fear they've committed the unforgivable sin of shirk

- Familial dishonor drives many in the Middle East to commit honor killings. Although there is no command in the Quran or hadith to carry out "honor killings," there are commands in the Quran to kill mischief makers, as well as plenty of commands in the *hadith* to kill apostates—and they are not limited to the Middle East.

- *Shirk*: the unforgivable sin in Islam; it is roughly equivalent to idolatry, placing something or someone in the position due to Allah

Reflection Questions

1. If you were to share the gospel message with a Muslim friend, what would you say?

2. As a Christian, how can you subvert the Muslim honor-shame paradigm, while also showing them what it means to be a true Christian?

3. What do both *Surah* 2:18b and Matthew 7:7–8 speak to? How might you use both to encourage a Muslim to pray for confirmation in order to believe?

Essay Question

1. Nabeel explains that the cost for Muslims accepting the gospel can be tremendous. Were any of the costs he listed surprising to you? Which ones did you resonate with the most? How can you be sensitive to these costs as you reach out to Muslims?

Quiz

1. (T/F) Muslims often risk everything to embrace the cross.

2. What are the costs for Muslims accepting the gospel?
   a) Immediately ostracized from community
   b) Rejection by friends and family; brings shame to family
   c) Fear they might be wrong

    d) Fear they've committed the unforgivable sin of *shirk*

    e) All of the above

3. What do Muslims lose by accepting the gospel?

    a) Relationships

    b) Their very life

    c) If they are wrong, the afterlife

    d) Everything

    e) All of the above

4. (T/F) Although there is no command in the Quran or *hadith* to carry out "honor killings," there are commands in the Quran to kill mischief makers, as well as plenty of commands in the *hadith* to kill apostates.

5. (T/F) Familial dishonor drives many in the Middle East to commit honor killings. However, these kinds of killings are limited to the Middle East.

6. According to the gospel, God:

    a) Loves us

    b) Lowered himself for us

    c) Suffered and died for us

    d) All of the above

7. The belief that someone other than Allah is God.

    a) *Shahada*

    b) *Shirk*

    c) *Salaat*

    d) *Sharia*

8. (T/F) The Quran teaches that Christians and Jews are deluded for thinking that God is their father. Instead, they are his creatures and should see themselves in that light.

9. "When my servants ask about me, I am near. I answer their prayers when they pray to me. So let them hear my call and believe in me, that they may walk in the right way." Where is this verse found?

    a) Matthew 7:7–8

    b) *Surah* 2:186

c) *Surah* 2:122
d) Matthew 10:32–33

10. "Ask and it will be given to you; seek and you will find; knock and the door will be opened to you. For everyone who asks receives; the one who seeks finds; and to the one who knocks, the door will be opened."

a) Matthew 7:7–8
b) *Surah* 2:186
c) *Surah* 2:122
d) Matthew 10:32–33

CHAPTER 10

Guided by the Hand of God

You Should Know

- One of the primary ways Muslims believe God communicates with them is through dreams; if God gives someone a dream, he will also provide the means to interpret it.

- *Assalamu alaikum*: a Muslim greeting, meaning "Peace be unto you!"

- It's important to remember what Jesus has called us to do with people who don't know him: live among them

- How to find Muslims: refugees; students; immigrants; look and pray

- How to witness generally: take a step forward; err on the side of discomfort; be hospitable; love them for their own sake; be transparent; and have humility in your walk

- How to reach Muslims specifically: be very insistent on your hospitality; be humble; don't serve pork or alcohol; serve tea; learn some of their language; pray regularly and practice spiritual disciplines

Reflection Questions

1. Nabeel lists a number of ways you can make contact with Muslims, from refugees to immigrants, from students to neighbors. To whom can you begin reaching out? If you don't know anyone, how might it look to begin making connections with these groups? With which of the groups in the previous question do you most resonate? To whom do you feel God laying on your heart to minister?

2. What are some of the ways we might inadvertently offend Muslims? How do you think we should respond when we do?

3. What do you think about Nabeel's encouragement to be joyful? Why do you think joy might be important when it comes to ministering to Muslims?

Essay Question

1. When it comes to reaching out to Muslims, it's important to remember that it takes time. How committed do you think you are to the long-term task of reaching out to Muslims and creating relationships with them? What are some practical steps you can take to reach out and minister to immigrant Muslims in your city?

Quiz

1. In what groups are we likely to find Muslims to whom we can reach out?
   a) Refugees
   b) Immigrants
   c) Students
   d) Neighbors
   e) All of the above

2. (T/F) When seeking to understand the Muslims to whom you reach out, it makes little difference whether they immigrated to your country or if they were born there.

3. If you meet a Muslim who was born in your Western country, then you should:
   a) Treat them like anyone else in your country.
   b) Treat them as if they were born in the Middle East.
   c) Treat them as if they were born in a Muslim country.
   d) Stay away from them.

4. It's important to remember what Jesus has called us to do with people who don't know him:
   a) Avoid them.

    b) Live among them.

    c) Convert them.

    d) Ban them.

5. The first thing we should do to reach out to Muslims is:

    a) Read the Old Testament regularly.

    b) Read the Quran regularly.

    c) Read Romans regularly.

    d) Read the Gospels regularly.

6. At the end of the day, if a Muslim we know doesn't become a Christian, we should:

    a) Try a different evangelistic technique.

    b) Go back to doing more research and return with better arguments.

    c) Continue loving them and being their friend.

    d) Stop trying and move on.

7. (T/F) It's not a problem to begin the discipleship process with Muslims before they have made a commitment to Christ. In fact, it's a very good thing, and it seems to be the biblical model.

8. What verse reflects God's master plan of evangelism?

    a) Matthew 5:1–7:29

    b) Mark 12:30–31

    c) Luke 4:18–19

    d) John 3:16–3

9. (T/F) Not only are we responsible for introducing the gospel to Muslims, we are also the ones who are supposed to convert them.

10. How can you ensure you are spiritually strong when you minister to Muslims?

    a) Intentionally follow Jesus.

    b) Don't be alone; talk about it with others.

    c) Learn and practice some spiritual disciplines.

    d) Have your church pray for you.

    e) All of the above

ANSWER KEY
1. E, 2. F, 3. A, 4. B, 5. D, 6. C, 7. T, 8. B, 9. F, 10. E

Notes

www.ingramcontent.com/pod-product-compliance
Lightning Source LLC
Chambersburg PA
CBHW010038040426
42331CB00037B/3307